Explore the Solar System

Mars

Revised Edition

WORLD
BOOK

a Scott Fetzer company
Chicago
www.worldbook.com

World Book, Inc.
180 North LaSalle, Suite 900
Chicago, IL 60601
USA

For information about other World Book publications, visit our website at **http://www.worldbook.com** or call **1-800-WORLDBK (967-5325).**

For information about sales to schools and libraries, call **1-800-975-3250 (United States),** or **1-800-837-5365 (Canada).**

Revised printing 2016

The Library of Congress has cataloged an earlier edition of this title as follows:
Mars.
    p. cm. -- (Explore the solar system)
  Summary: "An introduction to Mars for primary and intermediate grade students with information about its features and exploration. Includes charts and diagrams, a list of highlights for each chapter, fun facts, glossary, resource list, and index"--Provided by publisher.
  Includes index.
  ISBN: 978-0-7166-9536-3
  1. Mars (Planet)--Juvenile literature. I. World Book, Inc.
QB641.M35 2010
523.43--dc22
                         2009029901

This edition:
ISBN: 978-0-7166-2552-0 (print)
Set ISBN 978-0-7166-2549-0 (print)

E-book editions:
ISBN 978-0-7166-1889-8 (EPUB3)
ISBN 978-0-7166-2473-8 (PDF)

Staff

Executive Committee
President: Jim O'Rourke
Vice President and Editor in Chief: Paul A. Kobasa
Vice President, Finance: Donald D. Keller
Vice President, Marketing: Jean Lin
Vice President, International: Kristin Norell
Director, Human Resources: Bev Ecker

Editorial
Manager, Annuals/Series Nonfiction:
  Christine Sullivan
Manager, Science: Jeff De La Rosa
Editor, Science: Will Adams
Administrative Assistant: Ethel Matthews
Manager, Contracts & Compliance
  (Rights & Permissions): Loranne K. Shields
Manager, Indexing Services: David Pofelski

Digital
Director of Digital Product Content Development:
  Emily Kline
Director of Digital Product Development:
  Erika Meller
Digital Product Manager: Lyndsie Manusos
Digital Product Coordinator: Matthew Werner

Manufacturing/Production
Manufacturing Manager: Sandra Johnson
Production/Technology Manager: Anne Fritzinger
Proofreader: Nathalie Strassheim

Graphics and Design
Senior Art Director: Tom Evans
Senior Designer: Isaiah Sheppard
Manager, Cartographic Services: Wayne K. Pichler
Senior Cartographer: John M. Rejba

Printed in China by Shenzhen Donnelley Printing Co., Ltd., Guangdong Province
4th printing June 2016

Picture Acknowledgments:
Cover front: NASA/JPL-Caltech/Cornell; Cover back: NASA/JPL-Caltech/UCLA.

© Carson Ganci, Design Pics/Alamy Images 50; © Astrofoto/Peter Arnold, Inc. 54; Marble sculpture, Museo Nazionale Palazzo Altemps, Rome (© Dagli Orti/The Art Archive) 49; Private Collection, Lauros-Giraudon/Bridgeman Art Library 46; ANSMET, Case Western University 43; G. Di Achille, University of Colorado 59; © Roger Ressmeyer, Corbis 15; ESA ©2007 MPS for ORIRIS 9; ESA/DLR/FU Berlin 20, 33; ESA/NASA/Martin Pauer 37; Granger Collection 46; © Calvin J. Hamilton 11, 31, 44; NASA 16, 24, 30, 33, 35, 41, 42, 57; NASA/JPL 23, 26, 38, 39, 52, 53, 58; NASA/JPL-Caltech/University of Arizona 18; NASA/JPL/MRO 26, 27; © Shutterstock 12.

WORLD BOOK illustration by Steve Karp 45; WORLD BOOK illustrations by Paul Perreault 6, 29.

Astronomers use different kinds of photos to learn about such objects in space as planets. Many photos show an object's natural color. Other photos use false colors. Some false-color images show types of light the human eye cannot normally see. Others have colors that were changed to highlight important features. When appropriate, the captions in this book state whether a photo uses natural or false color.

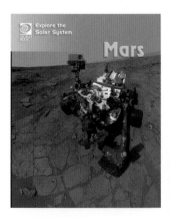

Cover image:
The Mars rover Curiosity appears in a self-portrait on the surface of the red planet.

Contents

If a word is printed in **bold letters that look like this,** that word's meaning is given in the glossary on pages 60-61.

Where Is Mars?

Mars is the fourth **planet** from the sun. The average distance between Mars and the sun is about 142 million miles (228 million kilometers).

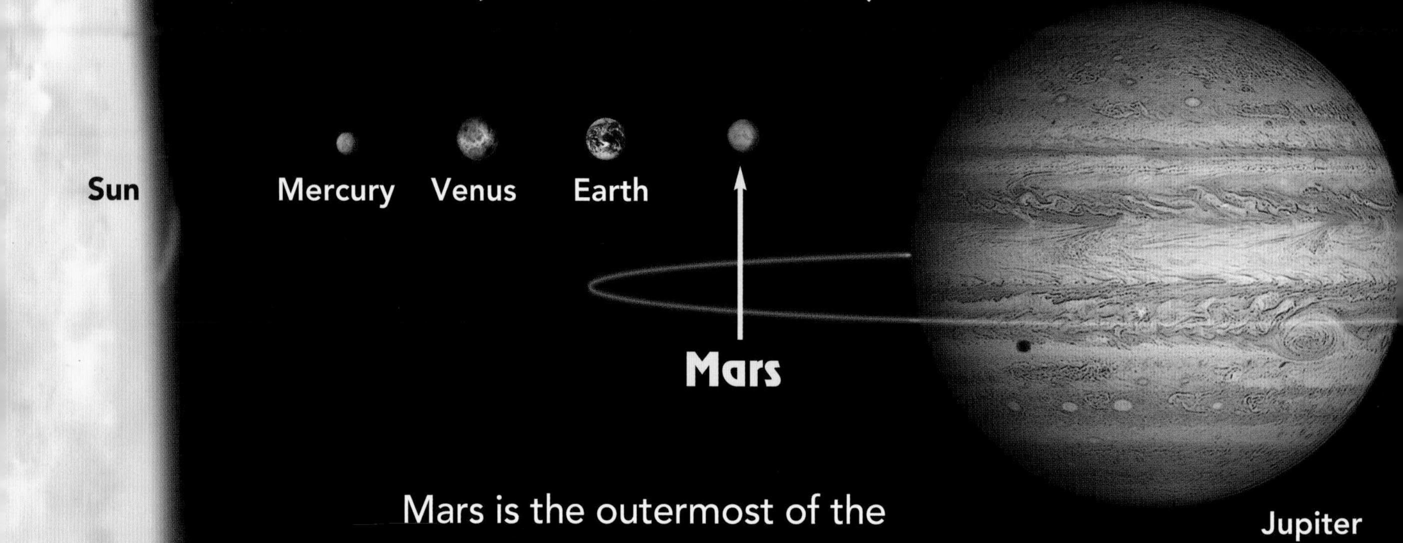

Sun   Mercury   Venus   Earth

Mars

Jupiter

Mars is the outermost of the four rocky inner planets. The other inner planets are Mercury, Venus, and Earth. The **orbit** of Mars lies between the orbits of Earth and Jupiter. Just past Mars, between the orbits of Mars and Jupiter, is the Main Belt. The Main Belt is a giant region of millions of **asteroids** that circle the sun.

The distance between Mars and Earth changes during the year, depending on the positions of the two planets in their orbits.

Mars's location in the solar system
(Planets are shown to scale.)

Saturn

Uranus   Neptune

Both planets follow **elliptical** (oval-shaped) orbits. However, Mars's orbit is a little more stretched out than the orbits of Earth and most of the other planets.

Sometimes, Mars and Earth come as close as about 35 million miles (56 million kilometers). That means that if a jet airplane could fly through space—at 500 miles (800 kilometers) per hour—it would take about eight years to reach Mars.

Highlights

- Mars is the fourth planet from the sun.
- Its orbit lies between the orbits of Earth and Jupiter.
- The average distance from Mars to the sun is about 142 million miles (228 million kilometers).
- The Main Belt lies between the orbits of Mars and Jupiter.

How Big Is Mars?

Mars is the second smallest **planet** in the **solar system.** It is larger than Mercury but smaller than Venus, Earth, Jupiter, Saturn, Uranus, and Neptune.

Mars is about half the size of Earth. Mars has a **diameter** of 4,221 miles (6,792 kilometers) at its **equator.** Earth has a diameter of 7,926 miles (12,756 kilometers) at its equator.

Fun Fact

For a small planet, Mars gets a lot of attention. More spacecraft have flown to Mars than to any other planet in the solar system.

Highlights

- Mars is the second smallest planet in the solar system. Only Mercury is smaller.
- The diameter of Mars is about half that of Earth's.
- The total land surface area of Mars is about the same as Earth's, because Mars has no bodies of water on its surface.

Although Mars is much smaller than Earth, the amount of dry land on the two planets is nearly the same. Oceans, lakes, and rivers cover about 70 percent of Earth's surface. The surface of Mars does not have any bodies of water. It is all land.

An artist's drawing comparing the sizes of Mars and Earth

Mars's diameter
4,221 miles (6,792 kilometers)

Earth's diameter
7,926 miles (12,756 kilometers)

What Does Mars Look Like?

From Earth, Mars appears as a bright, reddish star in the night sky. When seen through a telescope, Mars looks more like Earth than any other **planet** in the **solar system.** Earth, however, appears blue when seen from space. The blue color comes from Earth's oceans. Mars is mostly reddish. The red color comes from iron-rich **minerals** in the Martian soil. The minerals contain iron oxide— better known as rust—which is somewhat red in color.

The surface of Mars also has darker, grayish patches. These patches are areas of bare rock. They sometimes seem to change in size, but that is because they become covered by blowing reddish dust.

Highligl

- From Earth, M a bright, redd night sky.
- Mars appears because the n soil contain irc we know as ru
- Mars also has ice at its north poles.

Mars in a natural-color photo

Mars has caps of **water ice** and *dry ice* (solid carbon dioxide) at its north and south poles. These two caps change in size over the course of a Martian **year.**

Like Earth, Mars has white clouds, but Martian clouds are much thinner than Earth's. Wispy clouds drifting over the Martian surface can sometimes be seen from Earth with a telescope.

What Is Mars Made Of?

A thick, rocky **crust** covers the outside of Mars. Beneath the crust is the **mantle,** a layer of rock so hot that it is probably partly **molten** (melted). Beneath the mantle, in the center of the **planet,** is a large metal **core.** Scientists believe the core of Mars is most likely made up of iron, nickel, and sulfur.

The Mars Global Surveyor, launched by the United States in 1996, carried instruments that helped scientists learn a little about the interior of Mars. Their findings suggested that the core of Mars was once molten and probably still is.

Within Earth, temperature differences between the mantle and the molten core help create currents in the core. These currents produce electricity and create a **magnetic field.** Mars does not have a magnetic field. Some scientists think that **asteroid** impacts early in Mars's history shut down its magnetic field. They think the impacts heated the mantle to nearly the same temperature as the core.

Highlights

- The outer layer of Mars is a thick, rocky crust.
- Beneath the crust is a mantle that scientists think is at least partly molten.
- The planet's core is most likely made of iron, nickel, and sulfur and may also be at least partly molten.
- Unlike Earth, Mars has no magnetic field.

Inside Mars

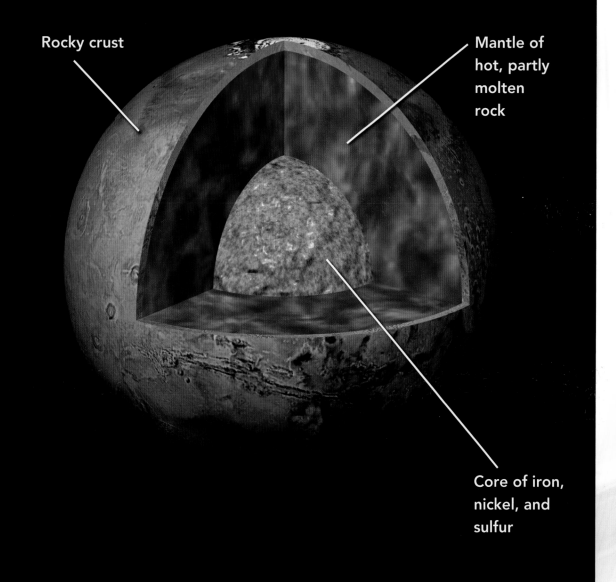

Rocky crust

Mantle of hot, partly molten rock

Core of iron, nickel, and sulfur

How Does Mars Compare with Earth?

In addition to being half the **diameter** of Earth, Mars has less **mass** (amount of matter). Mars also has less **density** (the amount of matter in a given space).

The **gravity** of a **planet** is related to the planet's size, mass, and density. So the force of gravity on Mars is less than it is on Earth. The force of gravity on the surface of Mars is only about one-third of that on Earth.

Weight depends on gravity, so a person on Mars would feel much lighter than he or she feels on Earth. Someone who weighs 100 pounds (45 kilograms) on Earth would weigh only 38 pounds on Mars (the equivalent of 17 kilograms on Earth).

Highlights

- Mars is smaller in diameter than Earth and has less mass, density, and gravity than Earth.
- The length of a year on Mars is about 687 Earth days.
- The length of a day on Mars is about 24 ½ Earth hours.
- Mars has two moons, compared with Earth's single moon.

How Do They Compare?

	Earth	Mars
Size in diameter (at equator)	7,926 miles (12,756 kilometers)	4,221 miles (6,792 kilometers)
Average distance from sun	About 93 million miles (150 million kilometers)	About 142 million miles (228 million kilometers)
Length of year (in Earth days)	365.25	686.98
Length of day (in Earth time)	24 hours	24 hours 39 minutes
What an object would weigh…	If it weighed 100 pounds (45 kilograms) on Earth…	…it would weigh about 38 pounds on Mars, the equivalent of 17 kilograms on Earth.
Number of moons	1	2
Rings?	No	No
Atmosphere	Nitrogen, oxygen, argon	Carbon dioxide, nitrogen, argon, oxygen, carbon monoxide, water vapor

What Is the Atmosphere of Mars Made Of?

Mars is surrounded by an **atmosphere** that is about 100 times as thin as Earth's atmosphere. The **pressure** of Earth's atmosphere is greatest near the **planet's** surface and decreases higher in the sky. Mars's atmosphere is so thin that near the surface, the pressure is lower than the pressure high in Earth's atmosphere.

Mars's atmosphere is made up mostly of a gas called **carbon dioxide.** The atmosphere also contains small amounts of water vapor as well as oxygen and other elements.

Clouds of frozen carbon dioxide and frozen water often form in the Martian sky. Photographs taken by space probes that have landed on Mars show that the sky is usually a pinkish color. The color comes from reddish particles of dust lifted into the air by Martian winds.

Highlights

- The atmosphere of Mars is much thinner than Earth's atmosphere.
- The Martian atmosphere is made up mostly of carbon dioxide.
- The Martian sky appears pink because winds on the planet carry reddish *particles* (tiny bits of matter) of Martian soil into the atmosphere.

Martian atmosphere

The atmosphere of Mars is visible in a natural-color photograph.

Fun Fact

Scientists knew a little about the atmosphere of Mars even before any spacecraft ever reached the planet. They had found Martian meteorites on Earth and discovered gas from the Martian atmosphere trapped inside.

Has the Atmosphere of Mars Changed Over Time?

Scientists believe that 3 billion to 4 billion years ago, the **atmosphere** of Mars was different than it is today. Mars probably had a much thicker atmosphere than it does today.

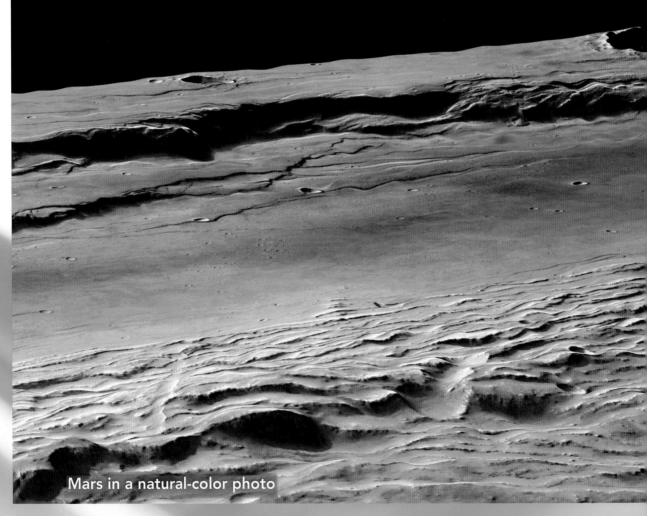

Mars in a natural-color photo

Photographs of Mars's surface taken by space **probes** show the remains of what appear to be riverbeds and channels. These features suggest that water once flowed across the **planet.** In 2004, NASA sent two robot **rovers**—Spirit and Opportunity—to Mars. In 2011, NASA sent another **rover**—Curiosity—to Mars. The rover analyzed the surface of Mars and discovered that the planet could once have hosted primitive life.

The evidence of flowing water on the Martian surface suggests that Mars probably also once had a thicker atmosphere. A thick atmosphere would have trapped heat near the planet's surface. The heat would have warmed the surface enough for water to remain in a liquid state.

Highlights

- Probes and NASA rovers have found evidence that water flowed on Mars at some time in the past.
- Scientists believe that Mars once had a thicker atmosphere that trapped heat at the planet's surface.
- Such an atmosphere would have allowed liquid water to flow on Mars.

Is There Water on Mars?

Mars has a lot of water, but most of it is frozen and lies at the poles or underground. If all the **water ice** (frozen water) at the Martian poles melted, it would cover the surface of Mars with a shallow ocean.

NASA's Mars Odyssey, launched in 2001, and the European Space Agency's (ESA) Mars Express, launched in 2003, have been exploring the **planet** from **orbit** for underground ice. Scientists were using radar, cameras, and special instruments to probe beneath the surface.

Highlights

- There is a lot of water on Mars.
- Most of the water is frozen and lies at the north and south poles and beneath the planet's surface.
- Some salty water can flow beneath the surface during warmer times of the Martian year.

In 2008, NASA's Phoenix Mars lander used its robotic arm to dig through the Martian soil. Beneath the soil were bright white patches of water ice. The patches gave scientists their first close-up photographic evidence of Martian water.

In 2015, scientists using information from NASA's Mars **Reconnaissance** Orbiter discovered that salty water can flow just below Mars's surface. The salts allow the water to remain liquid even below normal freezing temperatures.

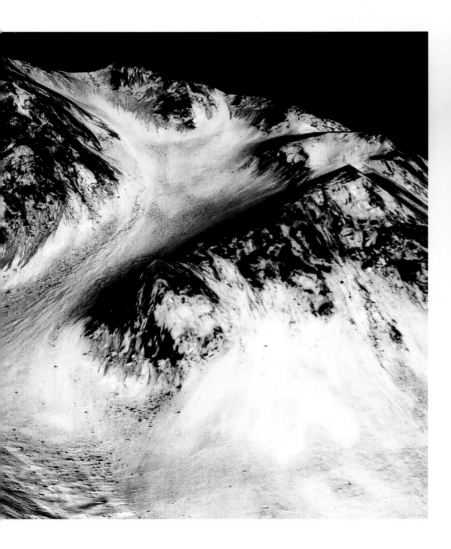

NASA's Mars Reconnaissance Orbiter took this picture of the slopes of Gale Crater on Mars. The dark, narrow streaks going down the sides of the mountains show recent flows of salty water just below the Martian surface.

Does Mars Have Rivers?

In 1971, NASA's Mariner 9 space **probe** photographed what looked like dry riverbeds on Mars. These photos were the first evidence that the **planet** had flowing water on its surface about 3 billion to 4 billion years ago.

A false-color photograph reveals a channel formed on Mars long ago by flowing water.

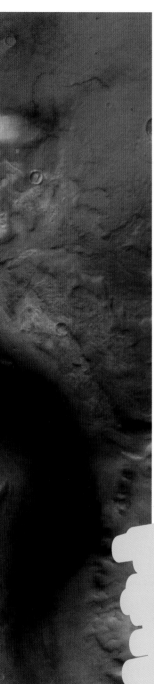

Some of these dry channels on Mars are as long as about 1,200 miles (2,000 kilometers) and as wide as 60 miles (100 kilometers). Scientists think these channels could have formed in floods on Mars. Millions of gallons of water could have flowed in streams, either on the surface or just below the surface. All of this water wore away the ground and made channels.

NASA space probes have found other signs that Mars had liquid water in the past. Small *gullies* (ditches) in the walls of **craters** show that water may have leaked from the ground within the past few million years. Other evidence shows that Mars may have once had large lakes or seas.

Highlights

- NASA space probes have found dry riverbeds on Mars, suggesting that the planet may have had rivers billions of years ago.
- Scientists have also found dry channels, which could have been formed by floods on Mars.
- The Martian surface shows evidence of large lakes or seas that may have existed long ago.

Was Mars Ever Like Earth?

Mars was warmer and more like Earth billions of years ago. Mars changed into the cold, dry place it is today because it lost most of its thick **atmosphere** (see page 16). As the atmosphere became thinner and thinner, it could no longer trap heat near the **planet's** surface. The surface cooled and all the water froze.

A planet's **magnetic field** helps protect its atmosphere from the *solar wind.* The solar wind is the constant stream of particles coming from the sun. The magnetic field around a planet pushes most of these particles away. When Mars lost its magnetic field (see

Seas may have covered much of Mars 3 billion years ago, as shown in an illustration based on information gathered by various spacecraft.

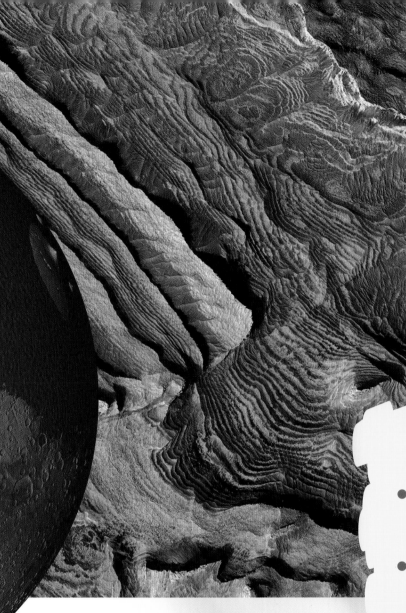

A photo taken by NASA's Mars **Reconnaissance** Orbiter shows layers in Martian rock. The layers contain bits of material that may have been deposited by flowing water.

Highlights

- Scientists think that Mars was more like Earth billions of years ago.
- Mars once had a thick atmosphere that became thin over time.
- When Mars lost its magnetic field, the solar wind blew most of its atmosphere away.
- Mars's atmosphere continues to get thinner today.

page 10), the solar wind particles began to hit the atmosphere. They ran into the gas molecules of Mars's atmosphere and knocked them into space. **Probes** have found that this is still happening today, and Mars's atmosphere gets thinner and thinner.

What Is the Weather Like on Mars?

The weather on Mars is cold, much colder than on Earth. High above the **planet's** surface, temperatures are below –200 °F (–130 °C). The average surface temperature on Mars is about –80 °F (–60 °C). Temperatures range from –195 °F (–125 °C) at the poles in winter to 70 °F (20 °C) at the **equator.**

When temperatures are at their lowest, water can freeze out of the air on Mars. Then, frosts, haze, or fog of **water ice** can form. Haze and fog are especially common on Mars early in the morning. The weather is too cold and the atmosphere is too thin for rain to ever fall. Frozen **carbon dioxide** sometimes falls as snow at the Martian poles.

Winds usually blow gently along the surface of Mars at about 6 miles (10 kilometers) per hour. But space **probes** have recorded wind gusts of up to 55 miles (90 kilometers) per hour. Dust storms with spinning winds—something like tornadoes—blow reddish dust around on Mars. The largest of these storms can cover the entire planet with a dusty haze.

Highlights

- The weather on Mars is much colder than on Earth.
- The average surface temperature on Mars is about −80 °F (−60 °C).
- It never rains on Mars, but snowflakes of carbon dioxide sometimes form at the poles.

A dust storm on Mars (left) and calm weather (opposite page), in natural-color photos

Does Mars Have Seasons?

Carbon dioxide gas breaks through a polar icecap during the Martian spring in a natural-color photograph. The gas carries red dust from under the surface with it, creating spidery patterns.

Highlights

- Mars has four seasons, just as Earth does.
- The Martian seasons occur because the planet is tilted on its axis, at about the same angle as Earth is.
- Seasons on Mars are twice as long as those on Earth, because it takes Mars about twice as long to travel around the sun.

Mars has seasons that change during the **year,** just as Earth does. Summer, autumn, winter, and spring occur because a **planet** tilts on its **axis,** the imaginary line running through the planet around which it **rotates** (spins).

As a planet follows its **orbit** around the sun, the amount of sunlight falling on different parts of the planet changes throughout the year. On Earth, for example, the Northern Hemisphere is warmer in summer because then it is tilted toward the sun. During this same time, the Southern Hemisphere is tilted away from the sun. At that time, the Southern Hemisphere experiences winter.

A season on Mars is about twice as long as a season on Earth. Mars has longer seaons because it takes almost twice as long as Earth does to orbit the sun.

Dark sand covering the floor of a crater reappears in spots as a layer of bright carbon dioxide frost that built up during the Martian winter thaws in the spring.

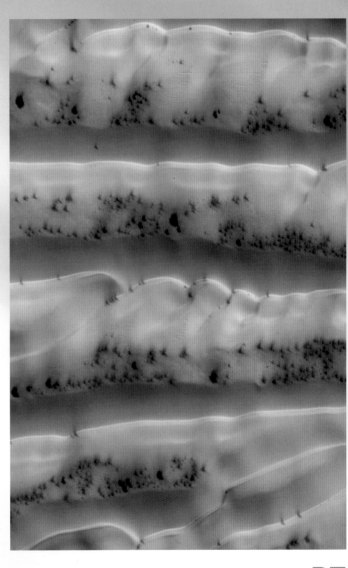

How Does Mars Move Around the Sun?

Mars **orbits** the sun in an **elliptical** (oval-shaped) path. Sometimes Mars comes as close as about 128 million miles (207 million kilometers) to the sun. Other times it is as far away from the sun as about 155 million miles (249 million kilometers).

Mars travels around the sun at a speed of about 15 miles (24 kilometers) per second. That is slower than Earth's speed of 18.5 miles (30 kilometers) per second. Because Mars travels farther and slower than Earth does, it takes about 687 Earth **days** for Mars to orbit the sun. That is the length of one Martian **year.**

Fun Fact

When NASA scientists work with the Mars rovers, they have to live on "Martian time" so they can send messages and receive data during the daytime. That means their day becomes 24 hours, 39 minutes, and 35 seconds long!

The Orbit and Rotation of Mars

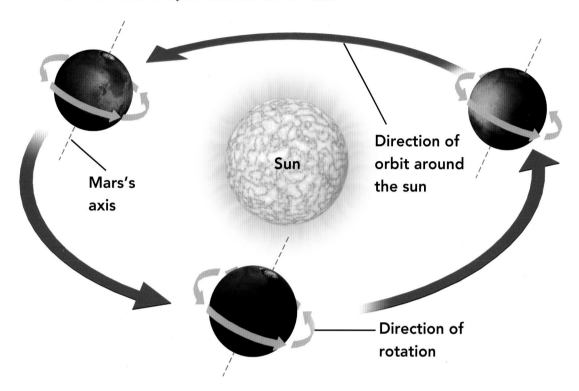

Sun

Direction of orbit around the sun

Mars's axis

Direction of rotation

The length of a day on a **planet** is the time it takes that planet to **rotate** (turn once) and return to the same position in relation to the sun. Mars rotates on its **axis** at a rate that is a little slower than the rate of Earth's spin. It takes Mars 24 hours 39 minutes and 35 seconds to rotate once on its axis. Like Earth, Mars rotates on its axis from west to east.

Highlights

- Mars travels more slowly around the sun than Earth does. Mars also travels farther in its orbit, because it is farther from the sun.

- One Martian year (the time it takes Mars to orbit the sun) is about 687 Earth days.

- One Martian day is 24 hours 39 minutes and 35 seconds.

What Is the Surface of Mars Like?

Although all of Mars has a solid surface, its northern half is very different from its southern half.

The northern half of Mars has flat plains that look similar to some of the deserts on Earth. The plains may have been smoothed out by water and flows of lava from volcanoes long ago. The southern half of Mars has many mountains and **craters.** Most of the craters were formed when **meteorites** slammed into the **planet's** surface billions of years ago.

The surface of Mars in a natural-color photograph

Rocks forming a dune-like pattern surround a crater on Mars in a false-color photo taken by the Mars Reconnaissance Orbiter.

Highlights

- The northern half of Mars is mostly flat, desert-like plains.
- The southern half has many more mountains and craters.
- Mars also has volcanoes, canyons, channels, and icecaps at its north and south poles.

Mars has many volcanoes, some of which are the largest volcanoes in the **solar system.** The volcanoes are wide and have long slopes, like the volcanoes that formed the Hawaiian Islands on Earth. Mars also has some of the largest and deepest **canyons** in the solar system.

Long, winding channels snake across the surface of Mars. They appear to be dry riverbeds. The north and south poles of Mars are covered with white icecaps.

What Is the Largest Canyon System on Mars?

The largest system of connected **canyons** on Mars is called Valles Marineris *(VAL uhs MAR uh NAIR uhs).* Valles Marineris makes Earth's Grand Canyon look small by comparison. The canyon system spreads along the Martian **equator** for 2,500 miles (4,000 kilometers)—about the distance from Philadelphia, Pennsylvania, to San Diego, California. The system was named after Mariner 9, the NASA spacecraft that discovered it in 1971.

Some of the canyons that make up Valles Marineris are up to 60 miles (100 kilometers) wide and 6 miles (10 kilometers) deep. Three canyons come together in the center of Valles Marineris to form a huge gap 370 miles (600 kilometers) wide. By comparison, Earth's Grand Canyon is 1 mile (1.6 kilometers) deep, extends about 277 miles (446 kilometers), and is 18 miles (29 kilometers) across at its widest point.

Highlights

- The largest canyon system on Mars is Valles Marineris.
- The system is 2,500 miles (4,000 kilometers) long and lies along the Martian equator.
- Valles Marineris was named for NASA's Mariner 9, the probe that discovered it in 1971.

Valles Marineris in a natural-color photograph made from a number of different images

Scientists think that Valles Marineris formed billions of years ago, when the **crust** of Mars split after it stretched too much. Water may have flowed through Valles Marineris long ago.

A section of Valles Marineris that is 1,060 miles (1,700 kilometers) long and 40 miles (65 kilometers) wide appears in a natural-color photo.

Mars 33

What Is the Largest Volcano on Mars?

Mars has some of the largest volcanoes in the **solar system.** The biggest of these is named Olympus Mons *(oh LIHM puhs mahnz).*

Olympus Mons is about 16 miles (25 kilometers) high and 370 miles (600 kilometers) wide. It is about three times as high as Mount Everest— the highest point above sea level on Earth. Early **astronomers** thought they saw white snow on the top of Olympus Mons. However, scientists now know that clouds make up the white material at the top of the volcano.

Three other large volcanoes are found near Olympus Mons, on a raised area called Tharsis *(THAHR sihs).* Tharsis lies along the **equator** of Mars.

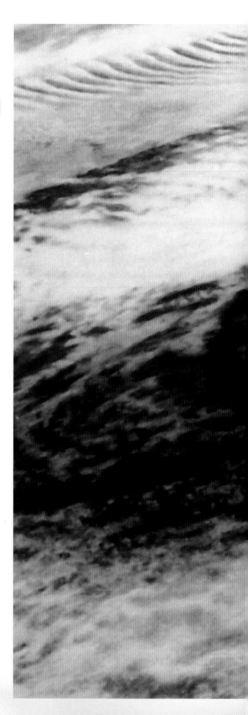

The largest volcano on Mars, Olympus Mons, in a false-color photograph

Scientists are not sure when the volcanoes of Mars last erupted. The volcanoes on Tharsis may not have erupted for more than 100 million years. But lava flows made by some other volcanoes may have occurred as recently as 2 million years ago. Scientists think that lava may still erupt from some Martian volcanoes from time to time.

Highlights

- The largest volcano on Mars is Olympus Mons.
- Olympus Mons lies near Tharsis, a large raised area on the Martian equator that also has three other large volcanoes.
- The volcanoes on Tharsis may not have erupted for more than 100 million years, but scientists think other volcanoes on Mars may still occasionally erupt.

What Is the Largest Crater on Mars?

Mars has one of the largest **craters** in the **solar system.** Hellas Planitia *(HEHL uhs pluh NIHSH ee uh)* is a Martian crater that is about as big as the Caribbean Sea on Earth. Hellas Planitia is 1,400 miles (2,300 kilometers) wide and 5.5 miles (9 kilometers) deep. The largest crater on Earth that we know of is only about 186 miles (300 kilometers) wide.

The craters on Mars formed when **meteorites** smashed into the **planet.** The rock surrounding many Martian craters looks as though it splashed out of the craters. That is because when the meteorites slammed into the surface, the crash produced heat. The heat melted underground ice to make a watery, splashy type of mud that later hardened into rock.

Craters on Mars are flatter and smoother than the craters on most other planets and **moons** in the solar system. These bodies have no real wind or weather. But wind is constantly wearing away the craters on Mars.

Highlights

- The largest crater on Mars is Hellas Planitia.
- The crater is 1,400 miles (2,300 kilometers) wide and 5.5 miles (9 kilometers) deep.
- Craters on Mars formed when the planet was struck by meteorites.

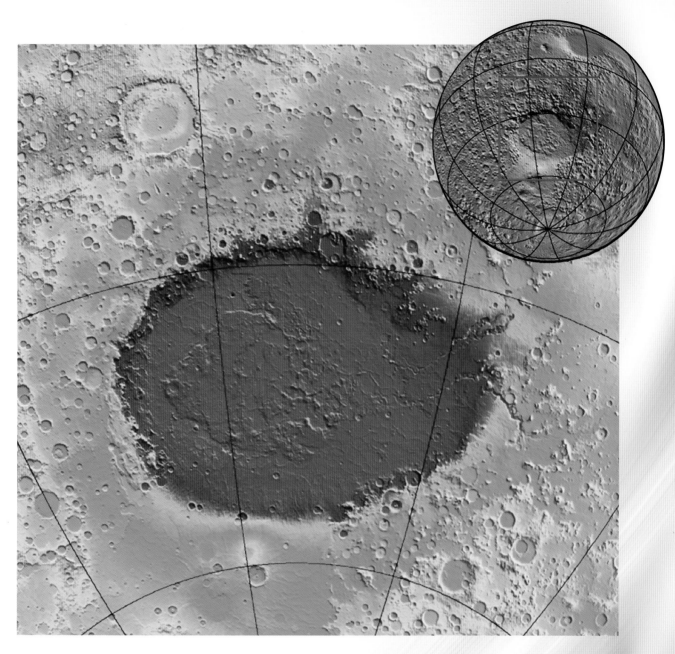

Hellas Planitia, the largest crater on Mars, appears on a false-color map of the planet. The colors are used to show the heights of different parts of the crater. The bottom of the crater appears purple. The walls of the crater are shown in blue. The area surrounding the top of the crater appears green and yellow. The red square on the globe shows the location of Hellas Planitia in the southern half of Mars.

What Are the Martian Poles Like?

The icecaps at the north and south poles on Mars are made mostly of **water ice.** In the Martian winter, **carbon dioxide** gas freezes out of the **atmosphere** to form a layer of frost that covers the poles. In spring and summer, the carbon dioxide returns to the atmosphere. This process causes the permanent icecaps to become larger in winter and smaller in summer.

In winter, the southern icecap can spread halfway to the Martian **equator.** In summer, the icecap almost

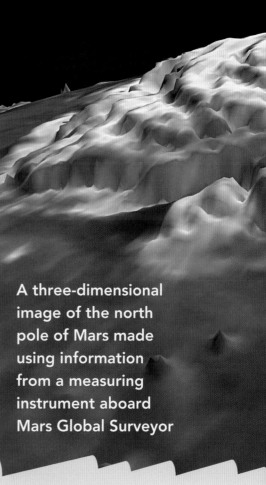

A three-dimensional image of the north pole of Mars made using information from a measuring instrument aboard Mars Global Surveyor

Highlights

- Icecaps cover the north and south poles of Mars.
- The icecaps are made of water ice covered by carbon dioxide frost.
- The Martian icecaps are larger in winter than in summer.
- The northern icecap is usually smaller than the southern one, because Martian summers are cooler in the north.

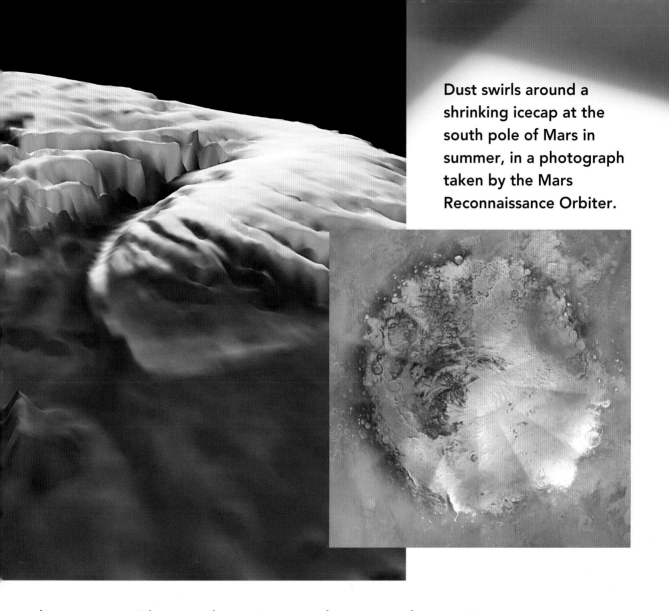

Dust swirls around a shrinking icecap at the south pole of Mars in summer, in a photograph taken by the Mars Reconnaissance Orbiter.

disappears. The northern icecap does not change in size as much as the southern icecap does. That is because summer temperatures in the northern half of Mars are much cooler than summer temperatures in the southern part of the planet.

Thick layers of dust and water ice surround the icecaps. These layers were probably deposited over long periods of time. Sand dunes also surround the icecaps on the northern half of the planet.

Does Mars Have a Face?

In 1976, a photograph taken by one of NASA's two Viking space **probes** showed what appeared to be a giant face on Mars. The face, which was about 2 miles (3.2 kilometers) long, seemed to have two dark eyes, a nose, and a mouth.

Since then, some people have claimed this photo showed that an intelligent civilization once existed on Mars. These people have argued that human-like creatures built the face long ago as some kind of monument.

In 1998 and 2001, NASA's Mars Global Surveyor space probe took sharper photos of the area. These photos showed that the "face" was just one of many natural rock formations rising from the northern plains of the **planet.** What happened to the eyes, nose, and mouth? They were just shadows caused by the way light was striking the hill when Viking photographed Mars in 1976.

Highlights

- One of the Viking space probes took a photograph of Mars in 1976 that seemed to show a face on the surface of the planet.
- More recent photos of the same area show that the "face" does not exist.

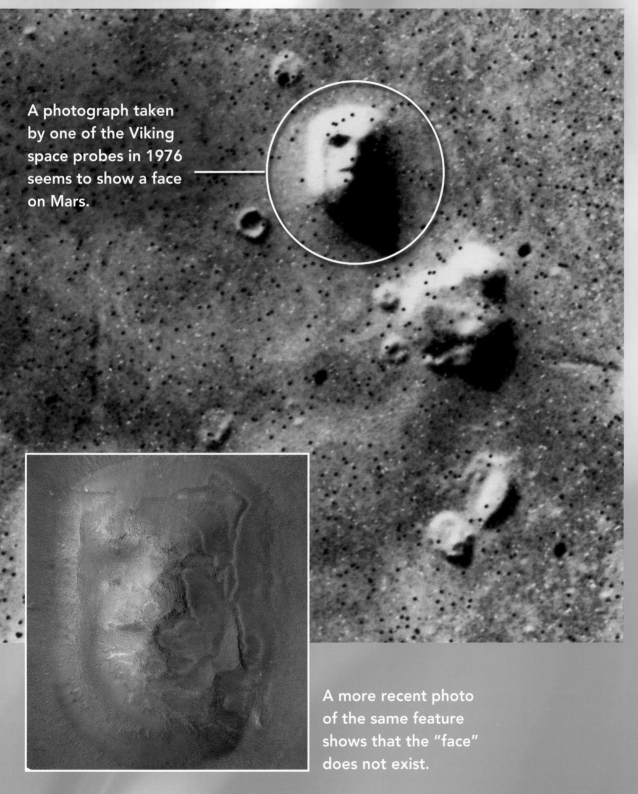

A photograph taken by one of the Viking space probes in 1976 seems to show a face on Mars.

A more recent photo of the same feature shows that the "face" does not exist.

Are There Pieces of Mars on Earth?

When **meteorites** slam into a **planet,** they sometimes hit the ground with so much force that pieces of the planet are blasted far into space. These chunks of rock can **orbit** the sun for millions of years. Eventually, the **gravity** of a nearby planet may cause the rocks to fall as meteorites. Scientists believe this has happened with pieces of Mars. More than 100 meteorites from Mars have been found on Earth.

A meteorite believed to have once been part of Mars

Scientists can usually tell if a meteorite came from Mars by comparing its chemical makeup to the chemicals that Viking space **probes** found in rocks on Mars. Martian meteorites have been discovered on all the continents of the world, but most have been found in Africa and Antarctica.

A technician at NASA's Johnson Space Center in Houston begins testing a meteorite found in Antarctica.

The largest known meteorite from Mars landed in the African country of Nigeria in October 1962. The rock, which weighed about 40 pounds (18 kilograms), crashed about 10 feet (3 meters) from a farmer who was chasing crows out of his cornfield!

Highlights

- More than 30 meteorites from Mars have landed on Earth.
- Scientists can identify a Martian meteorite by comparing its chemicals with those in rocks found by the Viking space probes on Mars.
- The largest meteorite from Mars to fall to Earth landed in Nigeria in 1962.

How Many Moons Does Mars Have?

The Martian moons Phobos (left) and Deimos (right) orbit Mars in an artist's illustration.

Mars has two small **moons** orbiting it. These moons are not round like Earth's moon. They have uneven shapes. They also have small **craters** covering their surface.

Some scientists think these moons were once **asteroids** that were captured by Mars's **gravity.** The asteroids then began to **orbit** Mars instead of the sun. Other scientists think the moons formed in orbit around Mars at about the same time as the **planet** formed.

Phobos (*FOH buhs*) is the larger of Mars's two moons. But at its widest, it is only 17 miles (27 kilometers) across. From the surface of Mars, Phobos can be seen rising in the west and setting in the east three times each Martian day. Deimos (*DY muhs*) is only 9 miles (15 kilometers) across at its widest. It is farther from Mars than Phobos.

Fun Fact

The moon Phobos orbits closer to its planet than any other moon in the solar system. It moves closer each day. In about 50 million years, Phobos will be broken apart by the force of Martian gravity. Its pieces might form a small ring around Mars.

Highlights

- Mars has two small moons, Phobos and Deimos.
- Phobos is the larger moon, and it is closer to Mars than Deimos.
- Some scientists believe that both moons were once asteroids and that the gravity of Mars captured them.

What Were Some Early Ideas About Mars?

Many people once thought that intelligent, human-like creatures lived on Mars. This idea was based on the way the **planet** looks through a telescope.

In 1877, an Italian **astronomer** named Giovanni (*juh VAHN ee*) V. Schiaparelli (*skee uh puh REHL ee*) said he saw a network of fine, dark lines running across the surface of Mars. He called these lines *canali*, which means *channels* in Italian. But *canali* was generally translated incorrectly as *canals*, which are structures built by people.

An engraving (left) shows the channels that Schiaparelli thought existed on Mars.

In the 1890's, the American astronomer Percival Lowell said he thought the canals had been constructed by an advanced Martian civilization. Other astronomers said the dark areas on Mars were crops planted by Martian farmers.

Today, scientists know that no canals exist on Mars. The images showing the so-called canals were dark and blurry. These unclear images led some scientists to misinterpret what they were seeing. The dark areas on Mars are just areas of bare rocks, not fields of crops.

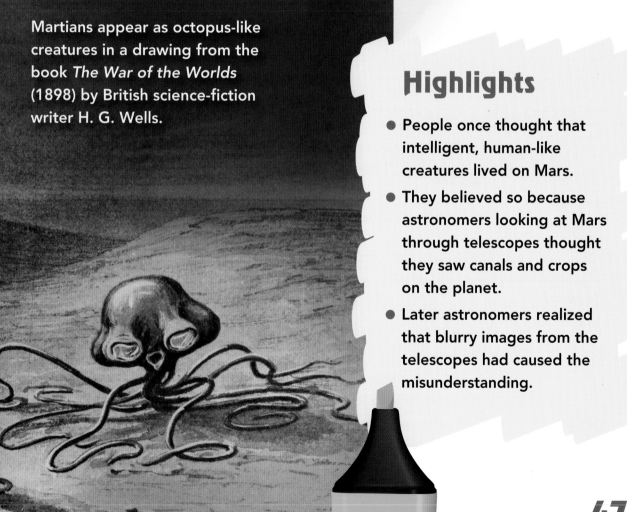

Martians appear as octopus-like creatures in a drawing from the book *The War of the Worlds* (1898) by British science-fiction writer H. G. Wells.

Highlights

- People once thought that intelligent, human-like creatures lived on Mars.
- They believed so because astronomers looking at Mars through telescopes thought they saw canals and crops on the planet.
- Later astronomers realized that blurry images from the telescopes had caused the misunderstanding.

How Did Mars Get Its Name?

Since ancient times, people have known Mars as the red "star" that moves from night to night in relation to other stars. All **planets** change their position in the sky from night to night, but Mars has always stood out because of its striking color.

The blood-like color of Mars led the ancient Greeks to name it after their god of war, Ares (*AIR eez*). Later, the ancient Romans named the planet after their own god of war, Mars.

Highlights

- The Romans named the planet Mars after their god of war.
- Earlier, the Greeks had named the planet Ares after their god of war, because the planet appeared blood-red in the night sky.
- The Romans named the month of March after Mars. Mars was once the god of farmland, and March was the time of year that the planting season began.

In Roman mythology, Mars was a god of farmland before he became the god of war. The Romans named the month of March after Mars, because farmers began planting their crops at that time. The Romans also thought of Mars as the father of Romulus and Remus, the legendary founders of Rome.

A sculpture of the Roman god Mars

Where Is Mars in the Night Sky?

Mars can be seen only at certain times of the year. During those times, Mars ranks as the third brightest **planet** in the sky, after Venus and Jupiter.

Fun Fact

On the night before Halloween in 1938, some people in the United States panicked because they believed that New Jersey was being invaded by Martians! They had been frightened by a radio play that actor Orson Welles produced based on H. G. Wells's novel *The War of the Worlds*.

Mars (opposite page) appears above the northern lights in a photo of the night sky.

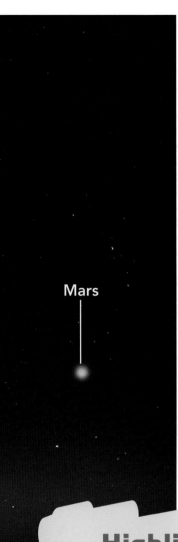

Mars

Mars appears to be a reddish star that slowly travels across the sky near the **ecliptic.** The ecliptic is an imaginary line. It represents the path that the sun appears to take in the sky to an observer on Earth as Earth **rotates** and **orbits** the sun. Earth's **moon** and the planets move across the sky near the ecliptic.

In some years, Mars is closer to Earth than in other years. During those times, dark markings can be seen on the surface of Mars as well as on one of its icecaps if the planet is viewed through a telescope.

Highlights

- Mars can be seen from Earth only at certain times of the year. At other times, its orbit takes it behind the sun.
- During times when Mars can be seen, it is often the third brightest planet in the sky. Only Venus and Jupiter are brighter.
- Through a telescope, Mars appears larger when its orbit brings it closer to Earth.

Which Space Missions Have Studied Mars?

NASA has launched more space-craft to Mars than to any other **planet.** In the 1960's, three Mariner space **probes** photographed parts of Mars that showed many **craters.** In the photos, Mars looked very much like Earth's **moon.**

A Mars rover explores the planet in an artist's drawing.

Highlights

- More NASA spacecraft have visited Mars than have visited any other planet.
- Viking spacecraft took the first photographs of Mars from the planet's surface in 1976.
- Wheeled robots called rovers have been traveling across the surface of Mars since the 1990's.

In 1971, however, Mariner 9 sent back photos that showed volcanoes, **canyons,** and dry riverbeds. In 1976, two Viking spacecraft landed on Mars. They took the first photos of Mars from the planet's surface.

Since the 1990's, many space probes have found signs that Mars once had liquid water on its surface. These probes include NASA's robot

NASA's Curiosity rover is the largest, most advanced robotic laboratory ever sent to the moon or another planet.

rovers, called Sojourner, Spirit, Opportunity, and Curiosity, which have traveled across the Martian surface. Curiosity also discovered clear evidence that Mars could once have hosted primitive life.

Orbiting spacecraft that have found evidence of water include NASA's Mars Global Surveyor and Mars Odyssey and the European Space Agency's Mars Express. NASA's Mars Reconnaissance Orbiter identified where water-related minerals are found and where water flows below the surface. NASA's Phoenix Mars lander explored the north polar area of Mars in 2008. The rover found **water ice** just inches beneath the rocky surface.

Will Astronauts Ever Visit Mars?

Many scientists think that a lot of important questions about Mars can be answered only by sending astronauts there. Scientists and engineers have already begun working to develop the technology needed for the journey.

The trip to Mars would be launched when Mars and Earth are relatively close to each other. Even then, it would take six to nine months—if not more—for astronauts to reach the red **planet.**

An artist's idea of how astronauts would explore Mars

The astronauts' spacecraft would have to be specially built to protect them from harmful radiation in space given off by the sun.

A team of astronauts would have to set up a place to live with the oxygen, water, and food they brought from Earth. The oxygen and water would probably be recycled, as they already are at the International Space Station. Fuel for the return trip to Earth might be made from chemicals in the Martian air and soil.

Maybe the astronauts would ride around in a **rover.** They could look for signs of water and life. They could also collect rocks to bring back to Earth.

Highlights

- Some scientists think we could learn a lot about Mars by sending astronauts there.
- It would take astronauts at least six to nine months to reach Mars.
- A spacecraft carrying astronauts to Mars would need to protect them from the dangerous radiation in space given off by the sun.

Will People Ever Colonize Mars?

Mars has captured people's imaginations for a long time. Many movies and novels have pictured the red **planet** as a place where creatures—someday maybe even people—could live.

Some scientists think that one day people might colonize—that is, live on—Mars permanently. This might be done by changing Mars into a planet more like Earth. Such a world-changing process is called **terraforming.**

In the future, scientists might be able to visit Mars and release gases into the **atmosphere.** The gases would then trap heat from the sun and warm the planet. An increase in temperature would cause the frozen **carbon dioxide** at the Martian poles to evaporate into the atmosphere.

Highlights

- Some scientists think that people could live on Mars and make the planet more Earth-like through a process called terraforming.
- The first step to making Mars livable might be to change its atmosphere.

A Mars base in an artist's drawing includes greenhouses for growing food and dirt-covered living spaces that would be protected from harmful radiation from the sun.

Over time, the extra carbon dioxide would help to make a thicker atmosphere that could trap even more heat, as Earth's atmosphere does. The surface might eventually become warm enough for the **water ice** on Mars to melt. Mars might then have rivers, lakes, and seas as it once did. Perhaps plants could be grown on a watery Mars. The plants would release oxygen into the atmosphere for animals and people to breathe.

Could There Be Life on Mars?

Most scientists believe that living things could not survive on the surface of Mars today. The **atmosphere** of the **planet** is too thin to block harmful ultraviolet (UV) rays from the sun. This radiation would probably kill any form of life on the Martian surface. Also, Mars is too cold for liquid water to exist on the surface. Life as we know it depends on liquid water.

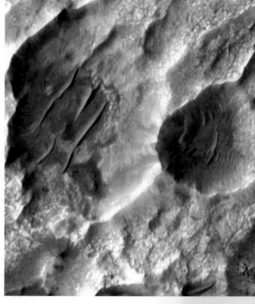

The Mars Odyssey space probe discovered salt deposits in many areas of the planet. On Earth, salt often preserves bacteria and other forms of life.

Highlights

- Most scientists do not believe that life as we know it can exist on the surface of Mars today.
- However, microbes might be able to exist below the planet's surface.
- We have no proof that there is or ever has been life on Mars.

Scientists think that **microbes** might exist underground on Mars. Under the surface, microbes would be protected from UV rays. There might also be liquid water underground on Mars.

Mars was much more likely to have had life billions of years ago, than it is today. That is because the planet was warmer then.

Still, Mars today definitely has two ingredients that scientists believe are necessary for life. The first is chemical elements, including carbon, oxygen, and nitrogen, that form the building blocks of living things. The second is a source of energy—either sunlight or heat from inside Mars. Mars may also have the liquid water essential for life.

Scientists used information about Mars collected by space probes to create an image of what the planet may have looked like more than 3 million years ago.

Glossary

asteroid A small body made of rock, carbon, or metal that orbits the sun. Most asteroids are between the orbits of Mars and Jupiter.

astronomer A scientist who studies stars and planets.

atmosphere The gases that surround a planet.

axis In planets, the imaginary line on which the planet seems to turn, or rotate. (The axis of Earth is an imaginary line through the North Pole and the South Pole.)

canyon A narrow valley with high, steep sides.

carbon dioxide A compound formed of carbon and oxygen.

core The center part of the inside of a planet.

crater A bowl-shaped depression on the surface of a moon, a planet, or an asteroid.

crust The solid outer layer of a planet.

day The time it takes a planet to rotate (spin) once on its axis and come back to the same position in relation to the sun.

density The amount of matter in a given space.

diameter The distance of a straight line through the middle of a circle or a thing shaped like a ball.

ecliptic The path that the sun appears to travel in one year.

elliptical Having the shape of an ellipse, which is like an oval or flattened circle.

equator An imaginary circle around the middle of a planet.

fossil The mark or remains of an organism that lived thousands or millions of years ago. Often fossils are preserved in rock.

gravity The effect of a force of attraction that acts between all objects because of their mass (that is, the amount of matter the objects have).

magnetic field The space around a magnet or magnetized object within which its power of attraction works.

mantle The area of a planet between the crust and the core.

mass The amount of matter a thing contains.

meteorite A mass of stone or metal that has struck the surface of a planet without burning up in that planet's atmosphere.

microbe A living organism so small that a microscope is needed to see it.

mineral An inorganic (nonliving) substance made up of crystals.

molten Melted.

moon A smaller body that orbits a planet.

orbit The path that a smaller body takes around a larger body, such as the path that a planet takes around the sun. Also, to travel in an orbit.

planet A large, round body in space that orbits a star. A planet must have sufficient gravitational pull to clear other objects from the area of its orbit.

pressure The force caused by the weight of a planet's atmosphere as it presses down on the layers below it.

probe An unpiloted device sent to explore space. Most probes send data (information) from space.

reconnaissance (rih KON uh suhns) To study a place.

rotate To spin around.

rover A vehicle for exploratory travel on the surface of a planet or moon.

solar system The sun and the planets and other heavenly bodies that orbit the sun.

terraforming The process of changing a planet or a moon's atmosphere, ocean, and climate to make it more like that of current-day Earth, so that human beings might colonize it.

water ice A term scientists use to describe frozen water, to distinguish it from ice that forms from other chemical substances.

year The time it takes a planet to complete one orbit around the sun.

For More Information

Books

Cars on Mars: Roving the Red Planet by
Alexandra Siy (Charlesbridge, 2009)

Destination Mars by Giles Sparrow (PowerKids
Press, 2010)

Mars by Elaine Landau (Children's Press, 2008)

The Mighty Mars Rovers: The Incredible Adventures of Spirit and Opportunity by Elizabeth
Rusch (Houghton Mifflin, 2012)

You Are the First Kid on Mars by Patrick O'Brien
(G. P. Putnam's Sons, 2009)

Websites

NASA's Mars Exploration Program
http://mars.jpl.nasa.gov/

NASA's Solar System Exploration: Mars
http://solarsystem.nasa.gov/planets/profile.cfm?Object=Mars&
Display=Kids

National Geographic's Science and Space: Mars
http://science.nationalgeographic.com/science/space/
solar-system/mars-article.html

Index